Plant Disc...

Liz Ray

Contents

Rigby®

A Harcourt Achieve Imprint

www.Rigby.com

1-800-531-5015

Think Like a Scientist

Plants play an important role in life on Earth because they provide food and shelter for people and animals, and they give off oxygen that we need to breathe.

Scientists have discovered many fascinating facts about the way plants grow and live. This book will show you how to think and work like a scientist to discover more about plants.

Many scientists use a system called the scientific method to help them create explanations for natural events. To use the scientific method, begin by asking a question based on something you observe. For example, seaweed grows in the salty water of the ocean. You know that plants need water to grow, but can a houseplant grow with salt water? You can answer this question by creating and conducting an experiment.

What questions could you ask about these plants?

Next gather information to help you understand your subject and design your experiment. Reading about the topic will help you figure out how to best find an answer to your question.

At this point you can make a hypothesis, a guess about what you think will happen in your experiment. For example, your hypothesis might be that a houseplant given salt water will not grow as much as a houseplant that has been given fresh water.

Now you are ready to conduct an experiment to test your hypothesis. In your experiment you might give one houseplant salt water and another plant fresh water. It would be important that you use the same kind of plants and give them the same amount of water and light. You would only change the type of water you give each plant.

    During the experiment, write down your observations. You will use these observations to draw a conclusion, or make a decision, about whether the results of your experiment prove your hypothesis to be right or wrong.

    Don't worry if your hypothesis was wrong. You learned valuable information that may help you make a new hypothesis.

Using the Scientific Method

Observe the world around you.

Research topics you find interesting.

Think of questions you would like to answer. Choose one and make a hypothesis.

Plan an experiment to test your hypothesis.

Do your experiment and write down your observations.

Use your observations to conclude if your hypothesis is correct.

Yes.
Tell everyone what you've learned!

No.
Plan another experiment.

Where Is the Light?

1

You already know that plants need light to grow, but what happens to a plant's growth if the light is hard to reach? You can conduct an experiment to answer this question.

You will need:

- 1 shoebox
- water
- scissors
- cardboard
- tape
- 1 sprouting bean plant in cup of soil

Procedure

1 Cut a hole in one end of the shoebox.

2 Cut three square pieces of cardboard and tape them to the inside of the box to make a simple maze. Make sure that it is possible to get from one end of the box to the other through the maze.

3 Put the cup with the sprouting plant in the box at the end opposite the hole.

4 Replace the lid and put the shoebox in a sunny window so that the hole is in the light.

5 Open the lid only to water the plant and check its growth.

Q **What did you observe?**

Which parts of this plant grew toward the light?

Results

As the plant grew, it bent around the cardboard maze like a snake to reach the light in a process called phototropism. Some parts of a plant, such as the stem, will bend toward a light source, while other parts of a plant will grow away from a light source.

Which part of the bean plant do you think grew away from the light? How can you find out?

A plant's leaves turn sunlight into food for itself, and phototropism helps the plant do this by making sure its leaves reach light. You can sometimes see the effects of phototropism in a thick forest or in other places where plants are crowded together and some are shaded from the sun.

What do you think would happen if a plant couldn't reach light? Can you set up an experiment to answer this question?

Why is this tree bent?

What could you do to make this plant grow straight?

Which Way Is Down?

In the last experiment, you saw the effect that light can have on the growth of a plant, but not all parts of a plant will grow toward light. There are other forces that can affect plant growth, too. The next two experiments will help you discover more about this.

You will need:

- 1 small plastic zippered bag
- 2 paper towels
- water
- 2 dried beans soaked overnight in water
- 1 clothes pin

Procedure

1 Fold two paper towels, wet them, and place them in the plastic bag.

2 Place the soaked beans in the center between the two paper towels so you can see the beans through the bag.

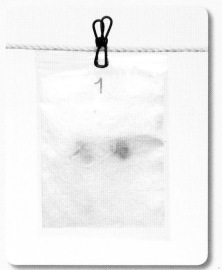

3 Press all the air out of the bag, and zip it closed. When you hold up the bag, the beans should stay in place. If they slip, try pressing out more air, or putting a tiny blob of clay under the beans to help keep them in place.

4 Hang the plastic bag on a bulletin board or clothesline and check it daily, adding water if the paper towels start to dry out.

5 When you see roots begin to grow down from the beans, turn the bag and hang it from its side.

Marking the bag will help you keep track of which side you already hung the bag from.

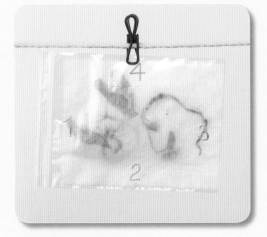

6 Observe the roots for several days, then turn the bag again and hang it from the bottom. After a few more days, turn the bag so it is hanging from the last side.

Q **What did you observe?**

What caused these roots to grow like this?

Results

As the seeds sprouted and grew, the roots grew downward. When you turned the seeds, the roots turned too, in order to keep growing down toward the center of the earth. This is known as geotropism, which is the effect of gravity on plant growth. You might see the effects of geotropism in plant roots that have had to grow around a large rock but then grew downward.

Many bulbs and some seeds are supposed to be planted with a specific end pointing down. What do you think might happen if you planted one of these bulbs or seeds upside down?

3 Reaching for Water

Water is important to a plant's life because a plant must have water to live, and it is the job of the plant's roots to find and carry that water to the different parts of the plant. But what will the roots do if the water is far away? This experiment will help you answer that question.

You will need:

- 1 shoebox
- 1 piece of plastic or wire mesh (like window screen)
- soil
- 8 dried beans soaked overnight in water
- 2 small bowls
- 1 spray bottle
- scissors
- water
- tape

Procedure

1 Cut two small holes (about 2 inches wide) in the bottom of the shoebox. Cut the holes at opposite ends of the box.

2 Cut two pieces of plastic or wire mesh to cover the holes in the shoebox. Tape the mesh inside the box over the holes.

3 Put 1 inch of soil in the box.

4 Place the soaked beans on the soil, spaced evenly along the length of the box.

5 Cover the beans with another inch of soil and water them with a spray bottle.

6 Fill one of the bowls with water, and make sure the other bowl is completely dry.

7 Rest the shoebox on the two bowls so that each hole is over a bowl.

8 As the beans grow, use the spray bottle to keep the soil moist but not too wet.

9 If water drips into the empty bowl, dry it completely. Look at the bottom of the box every day for about two weeks.

Q What did you observe?

Results

You saw the roots above the bowl grow down toward the center of the earth as well as toward the water. The roots over the empty

bowl also began growing downward. But when they found no water, they may have had to grow sideways, or even to turn and grow back into the soil in search of water there. This growth toward water is called hydrotropism.

Think about the beans that were not near one of the holes in the box. Which direction do you think their roots grew? How can you find out?

The desert is a good place to see roots affected by hydrotropism. Many plants that grow in the desert have very long roots spread over a large area, and they grow close to the surface instead of downward. That way they can collect as much rainwater as possible.

How do you think this plant gets the water it needs?

19

4 Drink Up!

You've seen how a plant's roots will grow in search of water, but how do water and minerals travel to the rest of the plant? This experiment will show you in a very colorful way!

You will need:

- 4 white carnations
- 5 jars
- 3 different colors of food coloring
- scissors
- water

Procedure

1 Fill each jar with water and add a different food coloring to each one.

2 Cut three flower stems so they are just a little taller than the jars.

3 Put one flower in each jar of colored water.

4 Cut off the very end of the fourth flower stem then split the stem in half so the flower is attached to two long stems.

5 Put one half of the split stem in one jar of colored water, and the other half of the stem in another jar of colored water. Leave the flowers in the colored water for 24 hours.

Q What did you observe?

What happened to the flower with the split stem? Why did this happen?

Results

As the plants sucked up water, they also sucked up the food coloring. Like juice or soda travels up a straw, the water and food coloring traveled up the stem to the flower, where they changed the color of the petals. Minerals in the soil travel in much the same way as the bits of food coloring did.

What do you think would happen if you put one of the colored flowers in a glass of plain water?

Although water and minerals won't turn a plant red or blue, you can still tell whether a plant is drinking enough. A plant that is not getting enough water will wilt, its leaves and flowers will droop, and its stem may bend. If the plant doesn't get enough water, eventually it will die.

Look for drooping houseplants or flowers. What do you think will happen if you water them?

Which plant looks like it needs water?

Escaping Water

5

You've seen how a plant takes in water and carries it to its different parts, but do you think a plant uses all the water it takes in? If not, what happens to the water it no longer needs? This next experiment will help answer that question.

You will need:

- 1 healthy growing plant
- 1 small plastic bag
- string
- water

Procedure

1 Tie the plastic bag around one leaf of the plant.

2 Water the plant and put it in the sun.

3 After several hours, check the inside of the bag.

Q What did you observe?

Results

You should see drops of water on the inside of the bag, and the air in the bag might look cloudy. This water traveled from the plant's roots and up the stem to the leaves. It was then released through tiny holes called stomata in the leaves. This process of losing water through a plant's leaves is called transpiration.

The water that plants give off through transpiration goes into the air (one plant can give off many gallons of water during a growing season). Although you can't see transpiration, you may be able to feel its effects. On a hot day, walk through a place where many plants grow. Does the air feel cooler there? Why do you think that might be?

stomata

An acre of corn can give off thousands of gallons of water a day.

Hairs or wax on the leaves of these plants keep them from losing water.

What do you think might happen if the stomata were covered so water could not escape from the leaves? Can you design an experiment to answer this question?

Some plants that live in very dry places have leaves that help them keep in moisture. Cactus spines are a special kind of leaf that do not give off as much moisture as broad, flat leaves do. Other kinds of plants may have hairy or waxy leaves that help them hold water in dry climates.

Bubbling Leaf

6

The last experiment showed you how plants lose water through their leaves. Do plants give off anything else through their leaves? This experiment will help you find out.

You will need:

- 1 healthy green leaf (with no brown spots)
- 1 clear glass jar or bowl
- water
- magnifying glass

Procedure

1 Look closely at the leaf with the magnifying glass. Do you see anything coming off the leaf's surface?

2 Put the leaf in the jar, and completely cover it with water.

3 Place the jar in sunlight.

4 After an hour, use the magnifying glass to look at the leaf again.

 **What did you observe?**

Results

You probably saw tiny bubbles forming on the leaf's surface and then rising off the leaf. These are oxygen bubbles escaping through the stomata.

Plants use sunlight, carbon dioxide, water, and minerals to make their food in a process called photosynthesis. During photosynthesis, plants give off oxygen through their leaves. We don't usually notice the oxygen when it goes into the air, but we can see the bubbles of oxygen underwater.

It's All Connected

carbon dioxide

oxygen and food

What do you think might happen if there were not enough plants to produce oxygen?

People and animals breathe in the oxygen that plants give off. We breathe out carbon dioxide, which the plants then use to make more food. This natural cycle shows how people, animals, and plants depend on each other. When we understand plants and how they grow, we can make sure to protect this natural cycle.

Think about the experiments in this book and what you discovered about plants. What questions did the experiments answer? What new questions do you have?

You may want to create your own hypotheses and experiments to answer these questions. And if more questions arise during those experiments, don't worry— it means you're thinking like a scientist!

Index